FOR A

Wonderful

HUSBAND

summersdale

FOR A WONDERFUL HUSBAND

Summersdale Publishers Ltd
46 West Street
Chichester
West Sussex
PO19 1RP
UK

www.summersdale.com

Printed and bound in China.

ISBN: 978-1-84953-291-4

Substantial discounts on bulk quantities of Summersdale books are available to corporations, professional associations and other organisations. For details contact Summersdale Publishers by telephone: +44 (0) 1243 771107, fax: +44 (0) 1243 786300 or email: nicky@summersdale.com.

25·12·14

To Mr Chard Gray

From Lady Veasa Gray

with all my love

x x x

*Men are all alike —
except the one you've
met who's different.*

MAE WEST

One good husband is worth two good wives, for the scarcer things are, the more they are valued.

BENJAMIN FRANKLIN

*My life really began when
I married my husband.*

NANCY REAGAN

Fascinating Fact!

The word 'husband' is from the Old Norse *husbondi* or 'master of the house'.

*The husband who wants
a happy marriage
should learn to keep
his mouth shut and his
chequebook open.*

GROUCHO MARX

You're
wonderful
because...

... you don't mind getting
your hands dirty.

Never feel remorse for what you have thought about your wife; she has thought much worse things about you.

JEAN ROSTAND

It is easier to be a lover than a husband for the simple reason that it is more difficult to be witty every day than to say pretty things from time to time.

HONORÉ DE BALZAC

You deserve
an award for:

Outstanding Service
as chief car-fixer and
spider-remover.

Getting to know someone is like investigating a crime scene where the culprit is constantly allowed to rearrange the evidence.

ADNAN MITHANI

The real act of marriage takes place in the heart, not in the ballroom or church or synagogue.

BARBARA DE ANGELIS

Marriage counsellors
recommend kissing
your partner for 20
seconds every day.
(And try not to look
at your watch.)

When a wife has a good
husband it is easily seen
in her face.

JOHANN WOLFGANG VON GOETHE

You're wonderful because...

... you can talk to Dad
about 'man stuff'.

The relationship between husband and wife should be one of closest friends.

B. A. AMBEDKAR

*The best proof of
love is trust.*

JOYCE BROTHERS

*Husbands are like fires —
they go out when they're
left unattended.*

CHER

You deserve
an award for:

Dedication to old-fashioned chivalry.

Only choose in marriage a man whom you would choose as a friend if he were a woman.

JOSEPH JOUBERT

A man in love is
incomplete until he
has married. Then
he's finished.

ZSA ZSA GABOR

Don't marry the person
you think you can live
with; marry only the
individual you think you
can't live without.

DR JAMES C. DOBSON

Studies have shown that the more a husband helps around the house, the lower the chance of divorce is.

*The faults of husbands
are often caused by
the excess virtues
of their wives.*

COLETTE

You're wonderful because...

... you enjoy eating
whatever I cook.

It's a wise husband who will buy his wife such fine china that she won't trust him to wash the dishes.

ANONYMOUS

My husband and I have figured out a really good system about the housework: neither one of us does it.

DOTTIE ARCHIBALD

You deserve
an award for:

Most Valiant Effort
at housework.

Marriage, n. A community consisting of a master, a mistress, and two slaves, making in all two.

AMBROSE BIERCE, *THE DEVIL'S DICTIONARY*

A successful marriage requires falling in love many times, always with the same person.

MIGNON MCLAUGHLIN

French-kissing requires using 34 facial muscles and 112 postural muscles. But why should the French have all the fun?

*What a happy and
holy fashion it is that
those who love one
another should rest
on the same pillow.*

NATHANIEL HAWTHORNE

You're wonderful because...

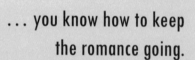

... you know how to keep
the romance going.

I do not want a husband who honours me as a queen, if he does not love me as a woman.

ELIZABETH I

Man's best possession is a sympathetic wife.

EURIPIDES

*Before I met my husband,
I'd never fallen in love. I'd
stepped in it a few times.*

RITA RUDNER

*You deserve
an award for:*

Best Dramatic
Performance when
answering, 'Does my
bum look big in this?'

An ideal wife is any woman who has an ideal husband.

BOOTH TARKINGTON

A kiss makes the heart
young again and wipes
out the years.

RUPERT BROOKE

I love you not because of who you are, but because of who I am when I am with you.

ROY CROFT

In certain parts of
ancient Greece, including
Athens and Sparta,
bachelors were excluded
from public office and
treated with scorn.

... *the one who, with a touch, can bring back the starlight and glow of years long ago.*

ALAN BECK ON THE DEFINITION OF A HUSBAND

You're wonderful because...

. . . you take real pride
in what you do.

Chains do not hold a marriage together. It is threads, hundreds of tiny threads which sew people together through the years.

SIMONE SIGNORET

*Love is what you've been
through with somebody.*

JAMES THURBER

You deserve
an award for:

Recognising the Importance of a big hug and a cup of tea.

There is no heaven like mutual love.

GEORGE GRANVILLE

If you press me to say
why I loved him, I can say
no more than because he
was he, and I was I.

MICHEL DE MONTAIGNE

One in ten husbands
don't know their
wife's date of birth;
don't worry, that
may be because she
keeps changing it.

A friend never defends a husband who gets his wife an electric skillet for her birthday.

ERMA BOMBECK

You're wonderful because...

... you don't complain about doing the driving.

There isn't a wife in the world who has not taken the exact measure of her husband... and knows him as well as if she had ordered him after designs and specifications of her own.

CHARLES DUDLEY WARNER

The best way to hold a man is in your arms.

MAE WEST

*A simple enough pleasure,
surely, to have breakfast
alone with one's husband,
but how seldom married
people in the midst of life
achieve it.*

ANNE MORROW LINDBERGH

You deserve
an award for:

Gourmet Chef of the Year in the category of Best Weekend Breakfasts.

You know you're in love
when you're willing
to share your cash-
machine number.

ELAYNE BOOSLER

And all for love, and nothing for reward.

EDMUND SPENSER

*A loving heart is
the beginning of
all knowledge.*

THOMAS CARLYLE

Researchers say that falling in love can induce a calming effect, and can raise levels of nerve growth factor, improving your memory — but only for the first year.

Your words are my food,
your breath my wine. You
are everything to me.

SARAH BERNHARDT

You're wonderful because...

... you do things with
confidence and determination.

I judge how much a man cares for a woman by the space he allots her under a jointly shared umbrella.

JIMMY CANNON

Being deeply loved by someone gives you strength, while loving someone deeply gives you courage.

LAO TZU

You deserve
an award for:

Heroic Patience during an incredibly long shopping trip.

*There is nothing nobler
or more admirable
than when two people
who see eye to eye
keep house as man and
wife, confounding their
enemies and delighting
their friends.*

HOMER

All women should
know how to take
care of children. Most
of them will have a
husband some day.

FRANKLIN P. JONES

The longest-married living couple are Karam and Kartari Chand of Bradford. Born and married in the Punjab region of India, they have been married for over 86 years.

I have learned that only two things are necessary to keep one's wife happy. First, let her think she's having her own way. And second, let her have it.

LYNDON B. JOHNSON

You're
wonderful
because...

. . . you're full of surprises.

Men have a much better time of it than women. For one thing, they marry later; for another thing, they die earlier.

H. L. MENCKEN

When a husband brings
his wife flowers for no
reason, there's a reason.

MOLLY MCGEE

When two hearts are one, even the king cannot separate them.

TURKISH PROVERB

You deserve
an award for:

Agreeing to Sit through a twelve-hour chick flick marathon with me.

Women are meant
to be loved, not to
be understood.

OSCAR WILDE

The reason husbands
and wives do not
understand each other
is because they belong
to different sexes.

DOROTHY DIX

Life without love is like a tree without blossoms or fruit.

KHALIL GIBRAN

Fascinating Fact!

If a man kisses his wife
every morning he will
live five years longer
than a man who doesn't.

Whatever our souls are made of, his and mine are the same.

EMILY BRONTË,
WUTHERING HEIGHTS

You're wonderful because...

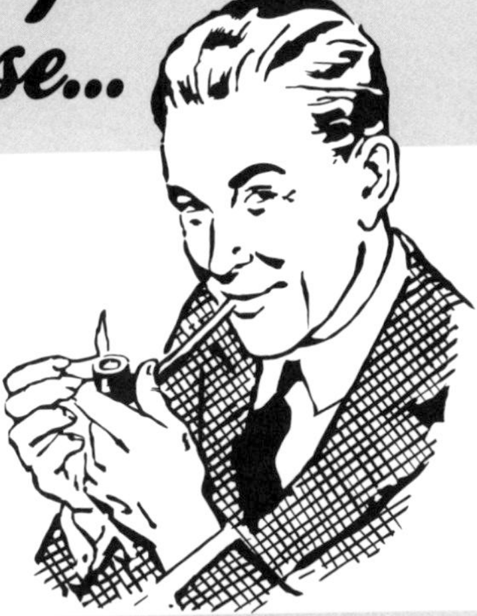

... you're dashing just
the way you are.

Marriage resembles a pair of shears, so joined that they cannot be separated; often moving in opposite directions, yet always punishing any one who comes between them.

SYDNEY SMITH

Love conquers all
things: let us too
surrender to love.

VIRGIL

You deserve
an award for:

Having a Place on your Shoulder where my head fits just perfectly.

I love being married. It's so great to find that one special person you want to annoy for the rest of your life.

RITA RUDNER

You're wonderful because...

... you're my rock.

If you're interested in finding out more about our gift
books follow us on Twitter: **@Summersdale**

www.summersdale.com